True or False?

Seasons

Daniel Nunn

Raintree is an imprint of Capstone Global Library Limited, a company incorporated in England and Wales having its registered office at 7 Pilgrim Street, London, EC4V 6LB – Registered company number: 6695582

To contact Raintree please phone 0845 6044371, fax + 44 (0) 1865 312263, or email myorders@raintreepublishers.co.uk. Customers from outside the UK please telephone +44 1865 312262.

Text © Capstone Global Library Limited 2013
First published in hardback in 2013
The moral rights of the proprietor have been asserted.

Edited by Dan Nunn, Rebecca Rissman, and Catherine Veitch
Designed by Joanna Hinton-Malivoire
Picture research by Ruth Blair
Production by Victoria Fitzgerald
Originated by Capstone Global Library
Printed and bound in China by Leo Paper Products Limited

ISBN 978 1 406 25157 9
16 15 14 13 12
10 9 8 7 6 5 4 3 2 1

British Library Cataloguing in Publication Data
Nunn, Daniel.
Seasons. – (True or false?)
508.2-dc23
A full catalogue record for this book is available from the British Library.

Acknowledgements
We would like to thank the following for permission to reproduce photographs: iStockphoto p. 10 (© Grady Reese); Shutterstock pp. 4 (© Smit), 5 and back cover (© Filip Fuxa, © Madlen), 6 (© jordache), 7 (© Nailia Schwarz), 8 (© 1000 Words), 9 (© Sofiaworld, © Sandra van der Steen (back cover)), 11 (© Maxim Tupikov, © Dominik Michalek), 12 (© Maxim Tupikov, © Dominik Michalek, © Artbox, © liseykina), 13 (© Patrik Mezirka, © s-ts), 14 (© Matt Hart), 15 (© Iwona Grodzka, © karam Miri, © Eric Isselée, © Coprid), 16 (© Delmas Lehman), 17 (© 1000 Words), 18 (© Andrew F. Kazmierski), 19 (© Diego Cervo, © PRILL Mediendesign und Fotografie), 20 (© A_Sh), 21 (© Bill Perry, © Ekaterina Pokrovsky), 22 (© Tan, Kim Pin).

Cover photographs reproduced with permission of Shutterstock (© Karam Miri (hat), © Eric Isselée (bird), © Coprid (goggles), © Rafel Olechowski (snow), Iwona Grodzka (bucket and spade)).

Every effort has been made to contact copyright holders of material reproduced in this book. Any omissions will be rectified in subsequent printings if notice is given to the publisher.

Contents

The seasons

A season is a period of time. The year is divided into four seasons. How much do **YOU** know about the seasons?

Summer

Summer is the coldest season of the year.

✔ **True or false?** ✗

✖ False!

Summer is the hottest season of the year. Summer is a great time to go to the seaside.

Autumn comes before summer.

✖ False!

Autumn comes after summer! Winter comes after autumn. Spring comes after winter. Then it's summer again!

Autumn

Squirrels store
nuts in the
autumn.

✓ **True!**

Squirrels store nuts in the autumn.
They hide them in autumn so they can
find them again in winter.

Some birds go on
holiday in the autumn.

✔ **True or false?** ✗

15

✔ **True!**

Some birds do go on holiday in the autumn! They fly away from the cold winter.

Winter

All trees are bare
and have no leaves
in the winter.

True or **false?** ✔ ✘

✕ False!

Some trees have no leaves in winter, but other trees stay green all year round.

Some animals sleep through the winter.

True or false? ✓ ✗

✓ True!

Some animals sleep through the winter. Hedgehogs sleep through the winter. This is called hibernating.

Winter around the world

Winter happens at the same time all over the world.

True or **false?** ✔ ✘

21

✖ False!

When it is winter in the United Kingdom and the United States, it is summer in Australia!

Can you remember?

Which animal goes on holiday in the autumn?

Which is the hottest season?

Which animal sleeps through the winter?

Look back through the book to check your answers.

Index

Activity

Make your own True or False game

Help your child to make their own Seasons: True or False game. Collect a selection of pictures showing the seasons from magazines. Mount each picture on card. Then with the child write a series of true or false statements about the seasons in the pictures on separate pieces of card. Put one statement with each corresponding picture. On the back of each picture write if the statement is true or false. For the game, read the statement out loud, ask the child if it is true or false, then turn over the picture to see if the child is correct. To extend the activity, ask the child to write the statements and whether they are true or false, and then ask you the questions.